Clip-Clue Puzzles

Clip-Clue Puzzles

Evelyn B. Christensen

Dale Seymour Publications

This book is dedicated to my wonderful family
and to the ultimate problem solver.

Project Editor: Joan Gideon
Production/Manufacturing Coordinator: Barbara Atmore
Design and Production: London Road Design

Published by Dale Seymour Publications, an imprint of the Alternative
Publishing Group of Addison-Wesley Publishing Company.

DALE
SEYMOUR
PUBLICATIONS
P.O. BOX 10888
PALO ALTO, CA 94303

Order Number DS21356
ISBN 0-86651-936-X

4 5 6 7 8 9 10-ML-99 98 97

Contents

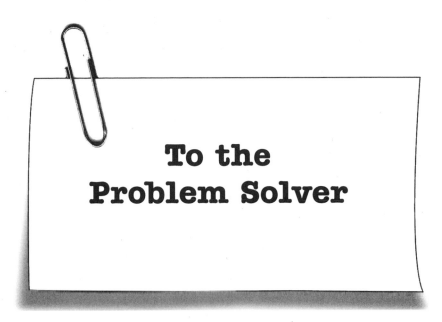

To the Problem Solver

The puzzles in this book have been great fun for me to create! I hope you will find them equally fun to solve. After you have worked some of them, you may want to try creating clip-clue puzzles of your own to share with other people.

Materials

As you read the clues, you can use paper clips to help you visualize the solution. For these puzzles you need 6 clips of each of the following 8 colors: white, pink, red, purple, blue, green, yellow, and orange. You do not absolutely need the clips to solve the problems, but having physical objects to rearrange often helps. (If clips are not available, you might try small rectangles of colored construction paper.) When you are solving a puzzle, it is easier if you leave the clips unlinked. A set of colored pencils will help you record your solutions.

Object

The object of a clip-clue puzzle is to use the clip colors listed at the beginning of the puzzle to make a chain that satisfies all the clues.

Clue Clarifications

1. Any clip that touches only one other clip is called an *end of the chain*.

2. Two chains are considered to be the same chain if one can be turned over or around to produce the other one. For example,

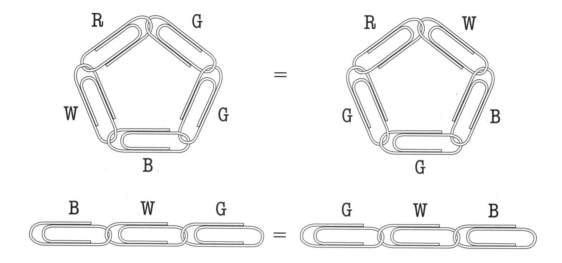

3. Chains that are shown in a polygonal shape (pentagon, hexagon, or octagon) should be solved as if they had been welded in that rigid shape. Two clips are *parallel* in a hexagonal or octagonal chain if they are directly across from each other.

4. A clip's *mate* is another clip of the same color. Clips of the same color are also called *color pairs*.

5. A *clip couple* consists of two connecting clips of the same color.
   A *clip triple* consists of three connecting clips of the same color.

When you are counting clip couples, you should count a clip triple as two clip couples. In the example below, *a* and *b* are one clip couple and *b* and *c* are another clip couple.

red (a)   red (b)   red (c)

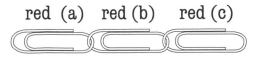

6. A *symmetric* chain is one whose colors would match if it were possible to fold the chain over on top of itself in the middle. (This folding may include folding a clip itself in half.) Every symmetric chain has a line of symmetry; the colors on one side of the line are the reflection of the colors on the other side of the line. These are examples of symmetric chains:

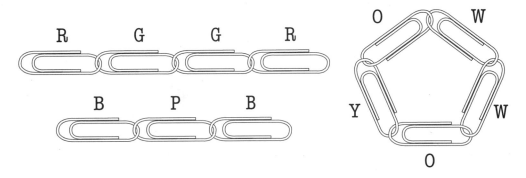

7. A chain forms a *repeating pattern* if the entire chain can be divided into two or more sections, all of which are identical, with the colors in the same order. These two patterns are repeating

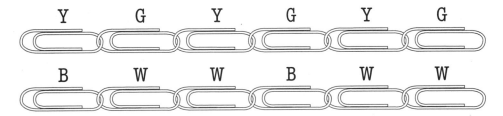

This is not a repeating pattern

8. Being *equidistant* from the middle or from the ends of the chain includes the possibility of being *at the middle* or *at the ends*.

9. Stating that a clip is *between* two specific clips does not exclude the possibility that another clip is also between those two clips. For example:

The blue clip is between the 2 red clips.

10. A statement about *a (red) clip* or *one (red) clip* does not exclude the possibility that one or more other clips of the same color might also fit the statement.
Example: The clue, "A red clip is at an end," is true for both the chain in number 9 and the chain in number 11. The statements "exactly one," "only one," and "just one" exclude the possibility of more.
Example: The clue, "Exactly one red clip is on an end," is true for the chain in number 11 but not for the one in number 9.

11. Additional relationships are illustrated by these examples:

"The blue clip is the second clip from the green one."
"The green clip touches two red clips."
"The blue clip touches a yellow clip."(We would not say,
"The blue clip touches two yellow clips.")

"The white clip is the fourth clip from *one end*."
"A blue clip is the fourth clip from *at least one end*."
"One color pair is separated by one clip, and the other color pair is separated by two clips."

Solutions

Verify your answers with the solutions beginning on page 95.

You are now ready to begin the puzzles. Have fun!

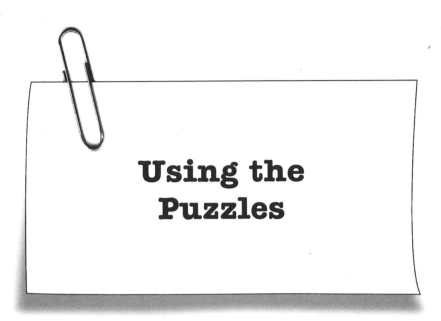

Using the Puzzles

Objectives

Clip-clue puzzles are, first of all, intended to be fun, but they are also designed to help people improve their problem-solving skills. Specific skills that are developed and exercised by these puzzle activities include:

- analyzing statements about relationships
- integrating two or more constraints on a system in the process of finding a solution
- generating more than one solution to a problem
- recognizing problems which are insolvable because of incompatible conditions
- discovering redundant information in the problem solving situation
- developing precise, sometimes genuinely creative, written statements about relationships
- evaluating a solution to determine if it meets all the given criteria

Age Level of Material

The activities in this book range in difficulty from easy to challenging and are appropriate for ages 8 to adult. Suggestions for using the material with the lower end of the age range are given below.

Using the Material with Younger Problem Solvers

In order for a problem-solving activity to be a mind-stretching and rewarding one for the problem solver, it must be challenging but not too frustrating. Some of the activities in this book can be quite challenging even for adults. If you are using the difficult puzzles with younger students, you may want to use one of these three suggestions to adapt your methods and the puzzles.

1. Use the puzzles with superfluous clues (puzzles 82–111) as plain clip-clue puzzles. If students want to try to find superfluous clues as an extra challenge, encourage them to do so, but do not expect the class as a whole to be successful with this challenge.
2. Use puzzles 112–157 as plain clip-clue puzzles, but warn the students that some will be impossible. If you want to tell them which puzzles have more than one solution, they will be more likely to find both solutions. (Otherwise, they will have the tendency to stop as soon as they find one solution.)
3. Working in groups is a good way for younger students to be successful with the more challenging puzzles in the book. Some suggestions for approaches to group activities are listed in the next section.

Strategies for Using the Puzzles in a Classroom

1. Make photocopies of the pages and give an appropriate number of puzzles to students, either individually or in groups, to solve during a specific class time or as homework. If you are sending the puzzles home with students, you may wish to consider the possibility of encouraging them to involve their families in the problem-solving process.

2. Post several of the easier puzzles or one of the harder puzzles on the bulletin board and provide a box for

students' solutions. Plan a time to discuss the results with the class or at least post a copy of the correct solutions.

3. Copy the puzzles on card stock and laminate them. Place these at an activity center where students who complete their regular assignments early can go and work. Solutions can be provided for them to check their own work, either on the back of each puzzle card or in an answer folder.

4. Use the puzzles as time-fillers when you have an extra few minutes at the end of a class period. You can show a puzzle on an overhead projector or display a sheet of newsprint on which you have previously copied a puzzle. If the clues are short you can dictate them to the students or write them on the board.

5. Use the first 51 puzzles to encourage cooperative problem solving among students. Here is one approach.
    • Select a puzzle.
    • Write each of the clues on a separate card without the clue numbers. Use the initial information (telling which clips to use) as an additional clue.
    • Form a group with as many problem solvers as you have clue cards. Give each problem solver a card. Give the group as a whole a set of clips and paper and colored pencils for recording their answer.
    • The group then works together to solve the puzzle.

    Since each person has necessary information to contribute, each person is an integral part of the problem-solving process. No one person can solve the puzzle alone.

    In a regular class you might have 6 or 8 such small groups working simultaneously. When one group finishes a puzzle, that puzzle can be passed on to another group.

6. If students have difficulty finding both solutions to clip-clue puzzles with insufficient clues, you can use another small group approach. Provide a copy of the puzzle for each member of the group and direct each one to work on the puzzle independently for 5 to 10 minutes first. Then have the members pool their solutions. If the group has still not discovered two solutions, they can then work through the puzzle together verbalizing their thought processes. Several students together are more likely to discover an incorrect assumption than a single student working alone.

7. For a group approach which can help students determine when a puzzle has a superfluous clue, follow these steps.
   • Select a puzzle with two clues.
   • Divide the class into two groups and give each group one clue.
   • Ask the students to work independently and find all the chains that satisfy their clues.
   • Get feedback from each group. List on the board, under each clue, all the chains that satisfy that clue.
   • Compare the two lists.
     a. If no chain is common to both lists, the puzzle has no solution.
     b. If exactly one chain is common to both lists, that is the unique solution.
     c. If exactly one chain is common to both lists and that chain is the only solution for one of the clues, the other clue is superfluous.
     d. If more than one chain is common to both lists, all the common chains are solutions.

If a puzzle has three clues, use a similar process but divide the class into three groups. Ask the first group to find all the chains that satisfy clues 2 and 3 simultaneously. The second group works with clues 1 and 3 simultaneously. The third group works with clues 1 and 2 simultaneously.

Creating Clip-Clue Puzzles

Although solving clip-clue puzzles is fun, I think creating them is even more fun. Solving a puzzle is largely an analytical, left-brain process, whereas developing a clip-clue puzzle allows me to draw on my right-brain creativity and incorporate it with the precision of left-brain relationships—definitely a satisfying experience.

After you have introduced clip-clue puzzles to your class at school or your children at home, you are likely to have at least some individuals who are eager to try creating their own puzzles. This is a wonderful opportunity for you to encourage students' creativity. To help them to be as successful as possible in their attempts, have them work at least some of the puzzles with insufficient clues (puzzles 52–81) before they try creating an entire puzzle. These puzzles will give students practice in writing clues that distinguish between just two specific chains.

Be encouraging, not critical, of student puzzle-writing attempts. If a clue is unclear, explain *why* it is unclear and ask them to rewrite it. If the puzzle was intended to have a unique solution, but somebody else discovers more than one solution, simply point out that the puzzle is similar to those with insufficient clues and ask the creator to add another clue or clues.

Give the creators a chance to share their puzzles with others. Puzzles generated by your students can be posted on the bulletin board, included on student worksheets, added to the set of cards at an activity center, or discussed in an all-class, problem-solving session. Having their puzzles included with the other puzzles can be very motivating for students.

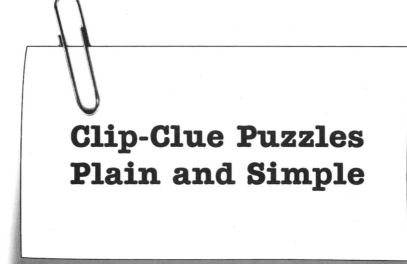

Clip-Clue Puzzles Plain and Simple

The clip-clue puzzles in this section require all the given clues to determine their solutions, and each puzzle has only one solution. If you think you have found two solutions, check to see if one chain can be turned over or around to look like the other one—two such chains are considered the same. Though all these puzzles are plain, some are not quite so simple.

If you have questions about the meaning of a clue, the information in "To the Problem Solver," pages 1–5, should provide clarification.

Clip-Clue Puzzle 1

Use 2 yellow clips and 1 green clip.

CLUE 1 The yellow clips touch each other.

Clip-Clue Puzzle 2

Use 1 red clip, 1 white clip, and 1 blue clip.

CLUE 1 Neither end of the chain is white.

Clip-Clue Puzzle 3

Use 1 orange clip, 1 blue clip, and 1 white clip.

Clue 1 The blue clip is the second clip from the orange clip.

Clip-Clue Puzzles Plain and Simple
©Dale Seymour Publications

Clip-Clue Puzzle 4

Use 3 purple clips and 1 blue clip.

CLUE 1 The blue clip touches 2 purple clips.

Clip-Clue Puzzle 5

Use 2 orange clips and 1 red clip.

CLUE 1 The chain is symmetric.

Clip-Clue Puzzle 6

Use 2 yellow clips, 1 orange clip, and 1 blue clip.

CLUE 1 Both ends of the chain are the same color.

Clip-Clue Puzzles Plain and Simple

©Dale Seymour Publications

Clip-Clue Puzzle 7

Use 2 blue clips and 2 green clips.

CLUE 1 The chain forms a repeating pattern.

Clip-Clue Puzzle 8

Use 2 orange clips, 1 purple clip, and 1 white clip.

CLUE 1 The white clip touches both orange clips.

Clip-Clue Puzzle 9

Use 3 red clips and 1 pink clip.

CLUE 1 The chain contains exactly 1 clip couple.

Clip-Clue Puzzles Plain and Simple

Clip-Clue Puzzle 10

Use 2 purple clips and 2 blue clips.

CLUE 1 A blue clip is between 2 purple clips.

CLUE 2 A purple clip is between 2 blue clips.

Clip-Clue Puzzle 11

Use 2 blue clips, 1 yellow clip, and 1 green clip.

CLUE 1 The green clip does not touch the yellow clip.

CLUE 2 The blue clips are next to each other.

Clip-Clue Puzzle 12

Use 2 red clips and 2 orange clips.

CLUE 1 The chain is symmetric.

CLUE 2 At least one end of the chain is red.

Clip-Clue Puzzles Plain and Simple

Clip-Clue Puzzle 13

Use 2 white clips, 1 pink clip, and 1 blue clip.

CLUE 1 One end of the chain is pink.

CLUE 2 The blue clip is between 2 white clips.

Clip-Clue Puzzle 14

Use 1 yellow clip, 1 red clip, 1 blue clip, and 1 white clip.

CLUE 1 The red clip and the white clip are in the middle.

CLUE 2 The red clip is between the white clip and the blue clip.

Clip-Clue Puzzle 15

Use 2 yellow clips, 1 green clip, and 1 blue clip.

CLUE 1 The blue clip touches the green clip.

CLUE 2 The green clip is between the yellow clips.

Clip-Clue Puzzle 16

Use 2 red clips, 1 white clip, and 1 blue clip.

CLUE 1 The white clip touches only 1 red clip.

CLUE 2 The blue clip is the third clip from a red clip.

Clip-Clue Puzzle 17

Use 2 orange clips, 1 yellow clip, and 1 red clip.

CLUE 1 The yellow clip is not between the orange clips.

CLUE 2 The red clip is between the orange clips.

Clip-Clue Puzzle 18

Use 2 orange clips, 1 green clip, and 1 white clip.

CLUE 1 An orange clip is between an orange clip and a green clip.

CLUE 2 The green clip is between a white clip and an orange clip.

Clip-Clue Puzzles Plain and Simple
©Dale Seymour Publications

Clip-Clue Puzzle 19

Use 2 pink clips and 2 red clips.

CLUE 1 A red clip is third from a pink clip.

CLUE 2 A pink clip is second from a red clip.

Clip-Clue Puzzle 20

Use 2 blue clips, 1 yellow clip, and 1 purple clip.

CLUE 1 The yellow clip touches a blue clip

CLUE 2 The purple clip touches a blue clip.

CLUE 3 The 2 blue clips touch each other.

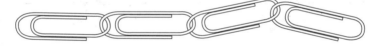

Clip-Clue Puzzle 21

Use 1 green clip, 1 white clip, 1 yellow clip, and
1 orange clip.

CLUE 1 The yellow clip is the third clip from the orange clip.

CLUE 2 The green clip does not touch the orange clip.

Clip-Clue Puzzles Plain and Simple
©Dale Seymour Publications

Clip-Clue Puzzle 22

Use 1 blue clip, 1 red clip, 1 white clip, and 1 yellow clip.

CLUE 1 The yellow clip is between the white clip and blue clip.

CLUE 2 The blue clip is between the white clip and red clip.

Clip-Clue Puzzle 23

Use 2 purple clips, 2 green clips, and 1 orange clip.

CLUE 1 The chain is symmetric.

CLUE 2 The orange clip touches a purple clip.

Clip-Clue Puzzle 24

Use 1 pink clip, 1 yellow clip, 1 blue clip, and 1 purple clip.

CLUE 1 The pink clip is between the blue clip and the yellow clip.

CLUE 2 The blue clip does not touch the pink clip.

Clip-Clue Puzzles Plain and Simple
©Dale Seymour Publications

Clip-Clue Puzzle 25

Use 2 orange clips, 2 red clips, and 1 yellow clip.

CLUE 1 The orange clips are between the red clips.

CLUE 2 The yellow clip touches just 1 orange clip.

Clip-Clue Puzzle 26

Use 2 blue clips, 2 orange clips, and 1 purple clip.

CLUE 1 The orange clips are on the ends.

CLUE 2 The purple clip does not touch either orange clip.

Clip-Clue Puzzle 27

Use 2 green clips, 2 blue clips, and 1 white clip.

CLUE 1 The chain contains 2 clip couples.

CLUE 2 The white clip touches both the other colors.

Clip-Clue Puzzles Plain and Simple
©Dale Seymour Publications

Clip-Clue Puzzle 28

Use 1 white clip, 1 pink clip, 1 blue clip, and 1 purple clip.

CLUE 1 The white clip does not touch the blue clip.

CLUE 2 The pink clip does not touch the purple clip.

CLUE 3 The blue clip does not touch the pink clip.

Clip-Clue Puzzle 29

Use 2 red clips, 2 blue clips, and 2 white clips.

CLUE 1 The chain contains 2 clip couples.

CLUE 2 The white clips are parallel to each other.

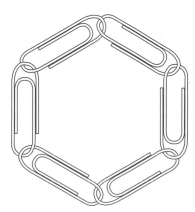

Clip-Clue Puzzle 30

Use 2 green clips, 2 yellow clips, and 1 orange clip.
CLUE 1 The orange clip does not touch either green clip.
CLUE 2 A green clip touches 2 yellow clips.

Clip-Clue Puzzle 31

Use 2 white clips, 2 blue clips, and 1 orange clip.
CLUE 1 The chain contains exactly 1 clip couple.
CLUE 2 Both blue clips touch the orange clip.

Clip-Clue Puzzle 32

Use 2 red clips, 2 pink clips, and 1 white clip.
CLUE 1 No clip touches its own color mate.
CLUE 2 No clip touches 2 clips of the same color.

Clip-Clue Puzzle 33

Use 1 yellow clip, 1 pink clip, 1 blue clip, and 1 purple clip.

CLUE 1 The blue clip is not between the pink and the purple clips.

CLUE 2 The pink clip is not between the purple and the blue clips.

CLUE 3 The pink clip does not touch the purple clip.

Clip-Clue Puzzle 34

Use 2 red clips,
2 blue clips,
and 4 white clips.

CLUE 1 Not all clips are parallel to their own color.

CLUE 2 No white clip touches white.

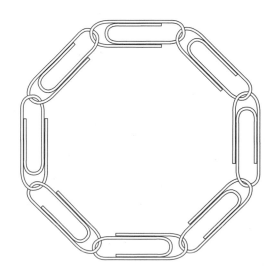

Clip-Clue Puzzles Plain and Simple

Clip-Clue Puzzle 35

Use 3 white clips, 2 orange clips, and 1 yellow clip.

CLUE 1 The yellow clip touches 2 different clip couples.

CLUE 2 A white clip touches an orange clip.

Clip-Clue Puzzle 36

Use 2 green clips, 2 yellow clips, and 2 blue clips.

CLUE 1 At least one end of the chain is green.

CLUE 2 Every clip touches its own color.

CLUE 3 A yellow clip is the fourth clip from a green clip.

Clip-Clue Puzzle 37

Use 3 blue clips, 2 purple clips, and 1 pink clip.

CLUE 1 Every blue clip is between 2 purple clips.

CLUE 2 The pink clip does not touch either purple clip.

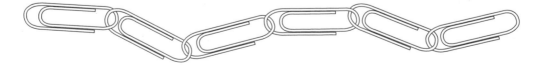

Clip-Clue Puzzles Plain and Simple

Clip-Clue Puzzle 38

Use 3 red clips, 2 green clips, and 1 white clip.

CLUE 1 Neither end of the chain is white.

CLUE 2 Two clip couples touch each other.

CLUE 3 The white clip does not touch either green clip.

Clip-Clue Puzzle 39

Use 4 orange clips and 4 blue clips.

CLUE 1 No clip is parallel to its color mate.

CLUE 2 Every orange clip touches at least 1 blue clip.

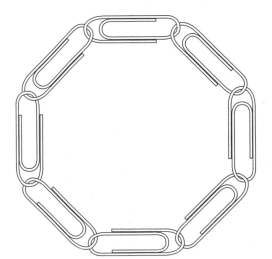

Clip-Clue Puzzle 40

Use 4 red clips, 1 yellow clip, and 1 blue clip.

CLUE 1 The chain has only 1 clip couple.

CLUE 2 The yellow clip is the third clip from the blue.

Clip-Clue Puzzle 41

Use 3 purple clips, 2 white clips, and 1 blue clip.

CLUE 1 The chain is symmetric except for the 2 end clips.

CLUE 2 The blue clip touches a white clip.

Clip-Clue Puzzle 42

Use 4 green clips and 2 blue clips.

CLUE 1 The chain forms a repeating color pattern.

CLUE 2 A blue clip touches only 1 green clip.

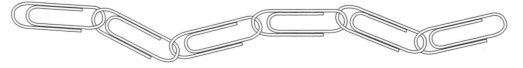

Clip-Clue Puzzle 43

Use 3 green clips, 2 pink clips, and 1 orange clip.

CLUE 1 No green clip touches another green clip.

CLUE 2 The 2 pink clips are equidistant from the ends of the chain.

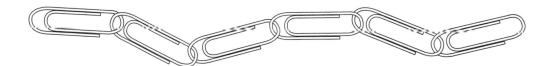

Clip-Clue Puzzle 44

Use 3 blue clips, 2 red clips, and 1 white clip.

CLUE 1 No clips of the same color are parallel.

CLUE 2 The chain is not symmetric.

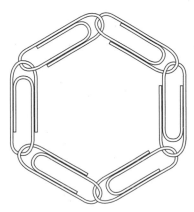

Clip-Clue Puzzles Plain and Simple

Clip-Clue Puzzle 45

Use 2 purple clips, 2 yellow clips, and 2 blue clips.

CLUE 1 Neither end of the chain is blue.

CLUE 2 A blue clip touches 2 purple clips.

CLUE 3 A clip is touching its color mate.

Clip-Clue Puzzle 46

Use 2 orange clips, 2 blue clips, and 2 white clips.

CLUE 1 The chain forms a repeating color pattern.

CLUE 2 A blue clip is fifth from the end.

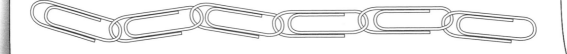

Clip-Clue Puzzle 47

Use 2 green clips, 2 red clips, and 2 blue clips.

CLUE 1 A blue clip is between 2 red clips.

CLUE 2 A red clip is between 2 blue clips.

CLUE 3 Neither end of the chain is blue or red.

Clip-Clue Puzzle 48

Use 2 orange clips, 2 pink clips, and 2 purple clips.

CLUE 1 Both an orange clip and a pink clip are the fourth clip from purple.

CLUE 2 The chain contains no pink clip that is equidistant from a purple clip and the other pink clip.

CLUE 3 The chain contains no clip couples.

Clip-Clue Puzzle 49

Use 2 red clips, 2 white clips, and 2 blue clips.

CLUE 1 The chain contains only 1 clip couple.

CLUE 2 A red clip touches 2 clips of the same color.

CLUE 3 One clip has 3 clips between itself and its color mate.

CLUE 4 A white clip is second from the end.

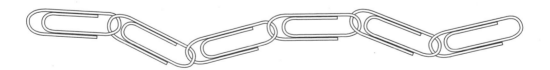

Clip-Clue Puzzles Plain and Simple

Clip-Clue Puzzle 50

Use 2 yellow clips, 2 orange clips, and 2 white clips.

CLUE 1 Neither end of the chain is orange.

CLUE 2 A yellow clip is third from the end.

CLUE 3 One clip separates one color pair, 2 clips separate another color pair, and 3 clips separate the third color pair.

Clip-Clue Puzzle 51

Use 4 green clips, 2 yellow clips, and 2 blue clips.

CLUE 1 Every green clip is parallel to a clip that touches green.

CLUE 2 The chain contains not more than 2 clip couples.

CLUE 3 The chain is not symmetric.

CLUE 4 A yellow clip is parallel to a clip that touches 2 clips of the same color.

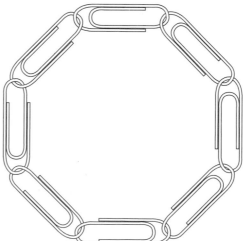

Clip-Clue Puzzles Plain and Simple
©Dale Seymour Publications

Clip-Clue
Puzzles with
Insufficient Clues

The clip-clue puzzles in this section do not give enough clues to have just one chain as a possible answer.

For each puzzle, study the clue or clues that are given. Figure out two different chains that satisfy all the given clues. (Remember that two chains are the same if one can be turned over or around to look like the other one.)

After you have found the two chains, record one chain in the first answer space and the other chain in the second answer space. Then write a clue that would make the first chain the only possible answer. Next write a different clue that would make the second chain the only possible answer.

For an extra challenge, try to write clues that still require all the given clues to solve the puzzle. This will be more challenging for some of the puzzles than for others. You may wish to work through the clip-clue puzzles with superfluous clues (puzzles 82–111) first to give you practice in determining when a clue is unnecessary.

Clip-Clue Puzzle 52

Use 4 yellow clips and 1 red clip.

CLUE 1 The red clip touches 2 yellow clips.

CLUE 2A _____

_____

CLUE 2B _____

_____

Clip-Clue Puzzle 53

Use 2 blue clips and 2 white clips.

CLUE 1 The two ends of the chain are not the same color.

CLUE 2A _____

_____

CLUE 2B _____

_____

Clip-Clue Puzzle 54

Use 2 green clips, 1 yellow clip, and 1 blue clip.
CLUE 1 Only 1 clip separates the yellow clip and the blue clip.

CLUE 2A_____

_____

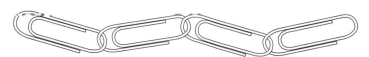

CLUE 2B_____

_____

Clip-Clue Puzzle 55

Use 3 purple clips and 2 blue clips.
CLUE 1 The blue clips form a clip couple.

CLUE 2A_____

_____

CLUE 2B_____

_____

Clip-Clue Puzzles with Insufficient Clues

Clip-Clue Puzzle 56

Use 2 orange clips, 2 white clips, and 1 red clip.

CLUE 1 The red clip does not touch 2 clips of the same color.

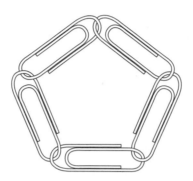

CLUE 2A _____

_____

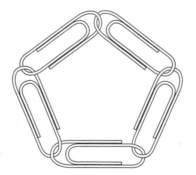

CLUE 2B _____

_____

Clip-Clue Puzzles with Insufficient Clues

Clip-Clue Puzzle 57

Use 3 blue clips and 2 pink clips.

CLUE 1 The middle clip in the chain is pink.

CLUE 2A _____

_____

CLUE 2B _____

_____

Clip-Clue Puzzle 58

Use 2 purple clips, 1 yellow clip, and 1 blue clip.

CLUE 1 The blue clip touches both a yellow and a purple clip.

CLUE 2A _____

_____

CLUE 2B _____

_____

Clip-Clue Puzzles with Insufficient Clues

Clip-Clue Puzzle 59

Use 2 green clips, 2 red clips, and 1 white clip.
CLUE 1 The chain has exactly 1 clip couple.

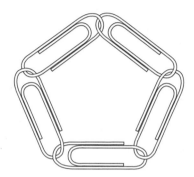

CLUE 2A _____

_____

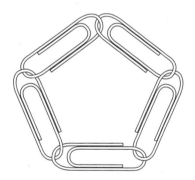

CLUE 2B _____

_____

Clip-Clue Puzzles with Insufficient Clues

Clip-Clue Puzzle 60

Use 5 orange clips and 1 white clip.
CLUE 1 Both ends of the chain are the same color.

CLUE 2A _____
_____

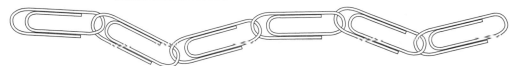

CLUE 2B _____
_____

Clip-Clue Puzzle 61

Use 2 purple clips and 2 blue clips.
CLUE 1 The chain is symmetric.

CLUE 2A _____
_____

CLUE 2B _____
_____

Clip-Clue Puzzles with Insufficient Clues

Clip-Clue Puzzle 62

Use 3 red clips and 3 white clips.

CLUE 1 No 2 clips of the same color are parallel.

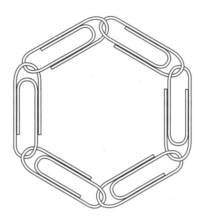

CLUE 2A _____

_____

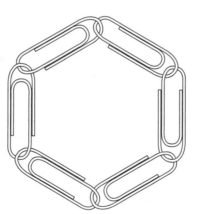

CLUE 2B _____

_____

Clip-Clue Puzzles with Insufficient Clues

Clip-Clue Puzzle 63

Use 2 green clips and 2 red clips.

CLUE 1 A red clip is between the 2 green clips.

CLUE 2A_____

_____

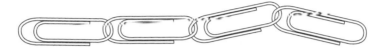

CLUE 2B_____

_____

Clip-Clue Puzzle 64

Use 3 orange clips and 2 white clips.

CLUE 1 Both ends of the chain are orange.

CLUE 2A_____

_____

CLUE 2B_____

_____

Clip-Clue Puzzles with Insufficient Clues
©Dale Seymour Publications

Clip-Clue Puzzle 65

Use 4 blue clips and 2 yellow clips.
CLUE 1 Only 2 blue clips are parallel.

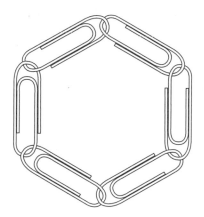

CLUE 2A_____

_____

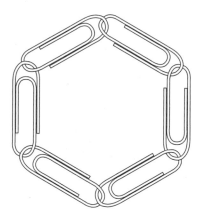

CLUE 2B_____

_____

Clip-Clue Puzzle 66

Use 2 yellow clips, 1 blue clip, and 1 orange clip.

CLUE 1 The first letters of the colors of 3 touching clips spell a word in the order they appear.

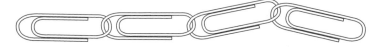

CLUE 2A_____

_____

CLUE 2B_____

_____

Clip-Clue Puzzle 67

Use 2 red clips and 2 blue clips.

CLUE 1 The chain is not symmetric.

CLUE 2A_____

_____

CLUE 2B_____

_____

Clip-Clue Puzzles with Insufficient Clues

Clip-Clue Puzzle 68

Use 4 red clips and 4 white clips.

CLUE 1 Every clip is parallel to a color mate.

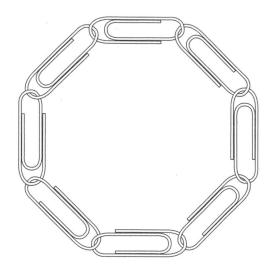

CLUE 2A_____
_____

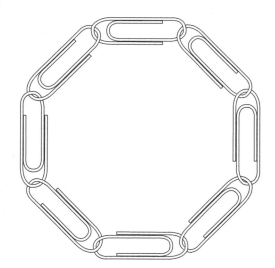

CLUE 2B _____
_____

Clip-Clue Puzzle 69

Use 4 green clips and 2 yellow clips.

CLUE 1 The chain forms a repeating color pattern.

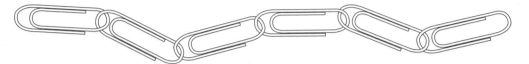

CLUE 2A_____

_____

CLUE 2B_____

_____

Clip-Clue Puzzle 70

Use 3 blue clips and 2 pink clips.

CLUE 1 The chain is symmetric.

CLUE 2A_____

_____

CLUE 2B_____

_____

Clip-Clue Puzzle 71

Use 5 orange clips and 3 red clips.
CLUE 1 Two red clips are parallel.

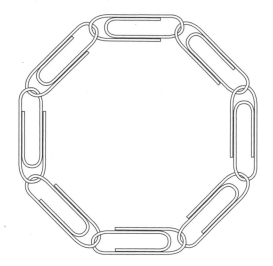

CLUE 2A _____

_____

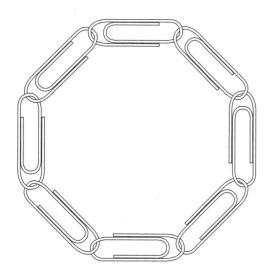

CLUE 2B _____

_____

Clip-Clue Puzzle 72

Use 3 blue clips, 1 orange clip, and 1 white clip.

CLUE 1 The ends of the chain are different colors.

CLUE 2 The orange clip touches 2 blue clips.

CLUE 3A_____

_____

CLUE 3B_____

_____

Clip-Clue Puzzle 73

Use 3 purple clips, 1 red clip, and 1 blue clip.

CLUE 1 The middle clip is not purple.

CLUE 2 The blue clip and the red clip do not touch.

CLUE 3A_____

_____

CLUE 3B_____

_____

Clip-Clue Puzzles with Insufficient Clues
©Dale Seymour Publications

Clip-Clue Puzzle 74

Use 5 blue clips and 3 yellow clips.
CLUE 1 Only 2 blue clips are parallel.
CLUE 2 The chain is symmetric.

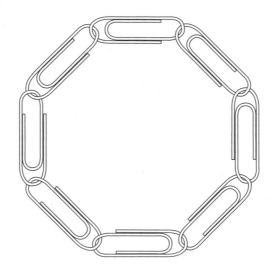

CLUE 3A_____

_____

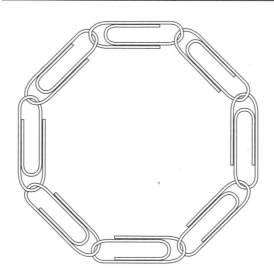

CLUE 3B_____

_____

Clip-Clue Puzzle 75

Use 3 orange clips, 2 white clips, and 1 pink clip.

CLUE 1 The pink clip is the fifth clip from one end.

CLUE 2 The chain contains a clip triple.

CLUE 3A_____

_____

CLUE 3B_____

_____

Clip-Clue Puzzle 76

Use 3 red clips, 2 white clips, and 1 blue clip.

CLUE 1 The chain contains no clip couples.

CLUE 2 At least one end of the chain is white.

CLUE 3A_____

_____

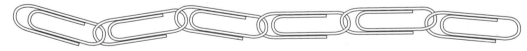

CLUE 3B_____

_____

Clip-Clue Puzzles with Insufficient Clues

Clip-Clue Puzzle 77

Use 4 blue clips and 4 green clips.
CLUE 1 No green clip touches 2 other green clips.
CLUE 2 Only 2 green clips are parallel.

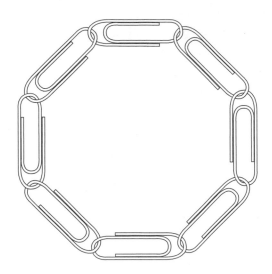

CLUE 3A _____

_____

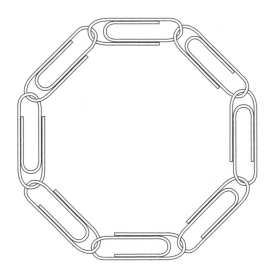

CLUE 3B _____

_____

Clip-Clue Puzzle 78

Use 2 purple clips, 2 blue clips, and 2 yellow clips.

CLUE 1 The purple clips do not touch yellow.

CLUE 2 Neither end of the chain is purple.

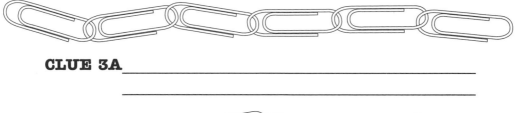

CLUE 3A_____

_____

CLUE 3B_____

_____

Clip-Clue Puzzle 79

Use 2 blue clips, 2 yellow clips, and 2 orange clips.

CLUE 1 At least one end of the chain is orange.

CLUE 2 The first letters of the colors of 3 touching clips spell a verb in the order they appear.

CLUE 3 The chain contains 1 clip couple.

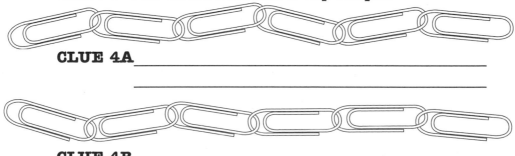

CLUE 4A_____

_____

CLUE 4B_____

_____

Clip-Clue Puzzle 80

Use 2 green clips, 2 pink clips, and 2 red clips.

CLUE 1 The 3 clips second, third, and fourth from either end contain a clip of each color.

CLUE 2 The red clip is separated from its color mate by exactly one clip.

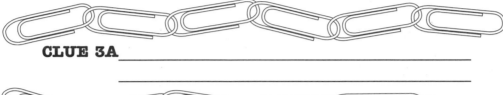

CLUE 3A_____

_____

CLUE 3B_____

_____

Clip-Clue Puzzle 81

Use 2 yellow clips, 2 orange clips, and 2 white clips.

CLUE 1 Each yellow clip is separated from an orange by only 1 clip.

CLUE 2 The white clips are equidistant from the middle of the chain.

CLUE 3 A yellow clip is closer to an end of the chain than either orange clip is.

CLUE 4A_____

_____

CLUE 4B_____

_____

Clip-Clue Puzzles with Superfluous Clues

Some of the clip-clue puzzles in this section have an extra clue that is not needed to find the unique solution to the puzzle. This superfluous clue adds no information to that already known from the rest of the clues.

For each puzzle find the unique solution, then check the clues to see if any of them were superfluous. If you find a superfluous clue, draw a circle around it. Not all the puzzles will have a superfluous clue.

Clip-Clue Puzzle 82

Use 1 red clip, 1 white clip, and 1 orange clip.

CLUE 1 One end of the chain is white.

CLUE 2 The red clip does not touch the white clip.

Clip-Clue Puzzle 83

Use 2 green clips and 2 purple clips.

CLUE 1 Neither end of the chain is purple.

CLUE 2 The purple clip touches its mate.

Clip-Clue Puzzle 84

Use 2 orange clips, 1 blue clip, and 1 pink clip.

CLUE 1 The blue clip is at one end of the chain.

CLUE 2 The pink clip touches both orange clips.

Clip-Clue Puzzle 85

Use 2 yellow clips and 2 orange clips.

CLUE 1 Each clip touches its color mate.

CLUE 2 A yellow clip touches an orange clip.

Clip-Clue Puzzle 86

Use 2 red clips, 1 white clip, and 1 blue clip.

CLUE 1 No clip touches 2 clips of the same color.

CLUE 2 The chain contains no clip couples.

Clip-Clue Puzzle 87

Use 3 green clips and 1 red clip.

CLUE 1 A green clip is between 2 green clips.

CLUE 2 The red clip is the third clip from a green one.

Clip-Clue Puzzles with Superfluous Clues

©Dale Seymour Publications

Clip-Clue Puzzle 88

Use 2 green clips, 1 blue clip, and 1 yellow clip.

CLUE 1 The yellow clip is between the blue clip and a green clip.

CLUE 2 The blue clip does not touch green.

Clip-Clue Puzzle 89

Use 2 white clips and 2 purple clips.

CLUE 1 Each half-end of the chain contains a clip of each color.

CLUE 2 The chain is not symmetric.

Clip-Clue Puzzle 90

Use 1 blue clip, 1 red clip, 1 orange clip, and 1 pink clip.

CLUE 1 The orange clip is between the red clip and the pink clip.

CLUE 2 The blue clip touches both pink and orange.

Clip-Clue Puzzles with Superfluous Clues

©Dale Seymour Publications

Clip-Clue Puzzle 91

Use 3 yellow clips and 1 blue clip.

CLUE 1 The blue clip touches 2 yellow clips.

CLUE 2 The chain contains a clip couple.

Clip-Clue Puzzle 92

Use 2 red clips, 1 orange clip, and 1 green clip.

CLUE 1 The orange clip is at one end of the chain.

CLUE 2 The green clip is the third clip from the orange clip.

Clip-Clue Puzzle 93

Use 2 orange clips, 1 blue clip, and 1 white clip.

CLUE 1 The blue clip is between the orange clips.

CLUE 2 The white clip does not touch the blue clip.

Clip-Clue Puzzles with Superfluous Clues
©Dale Seymour Publications

Clip-Clue Puzzle 94

Use 4 purple clips and 1 orange clip.

CLUE 1 The orange clip touches 2 purple clips.

CLUE 2 The chain is symmetric.

Clip-Clue Puzzle 95

Use 5 green clips and 3 blue clips.

CLUE 1 The chain contains no clip triples.

CLUE 2 Two green clips are parallel.

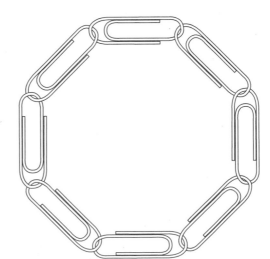

Clip-Clue Puzzle 96

Use 3 orange clips and 3 yellow clips.

CLUE 1 The middle 2 clips are not the same color.

CLUE 2 At least 1 end of the chain is yellow.

CLUE 3 The chain has at least 3 clip couples.

Clip-Clue Puzzle 97

Use 3 red clips, 2 white clips, and 1 pink clip.

CLUE 1 A red clip touches a pink clip.

CLUE 2 The white clips are equidistant from the ends.

CLUE 3 The chain contains no clip couples.

Clip-Clue Puzzle 98

Use 2 yellow clips, 1 white clip, and 1 blue clip.

CLUE 1 A yellow clip is between the white clip and the other yellow clip.

CLUE 2 Neither end of the chain is blue.

CLUE 3 A yellow clip touches a white clip.

Clip-Clue Puzzle 99

Use 4 green clips and 2 orange clips.
CLUE 1 The chain contains only 1 clip couple.
CLUE 2 The chain forms a repeating color pattern.
CLUE 3 A green clip is the third clip from at least one end.

Clip-Clue Puzzle 100

Use 2 red clips, 2 white clips, and 2 blue clips.
CLUE 1 Neither blue clip touches red.
CLUE 2 The chain contains 2 clip couples.
CLUE 3 Both a white clip and a blue clip are fourth from the end.

Clip-Clue Puzzle 101

Use 3 purple clips, 2 red clips, and 1 pink clip.
CLUE 1 The ends of the chain are the same color.
CLUE 2 The chain contains at least 1 clip couple.
CLUE 3 The red clips are equidistant from the pink clip.

Clip-Clue Puzzle 102

Use 2 blue clips, 2 green clips, and 2 yellow clips.

CLUE 1 The chain contains 1 clip couple.

CLUE 2 Neither end of the chain is blue.

CLUE 3 The clip on each end is separated from its color mate by exactly 3 clips.

Clip-Clue Puzzle 103

Use 3 orange clips and 5 yellow clips.

CLUE 1 The chain contains exactly 4 clip couples.

CLUE 2 Two orange clips are parallel.

CLUE 3 An orange clip touches 2 yellow clips.

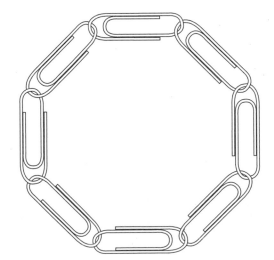

Clip-Clue Puzzles with Superfluous Clues

Clip-Clue Puzzle 104

Use 2 orange clips, 2 blue clips, 1 pink clip, and 1 green clip.
CLUE 1 The pink clip touches 2 clips of the same color.
CLUE 2 Both ends of the chain are the same color.
CLUE 3 The green clip is between blue and pink.

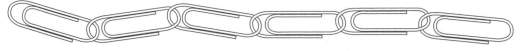

Clip-Clue Puzzle 105

Use 2 red clips, 2 blue clips, and 1 white clip.
CLUE 1 One clip is the third clip from its color mate.
CLUE 2 A blue clip is the second clip from at least one end of the chain.
CLUE 3 A blue clip touches 2 red.

Clip-Clue Puzzle 106

Use 2 pink clips, 2 purple clips, and 2 red clips.
CLUE 1 At least 1 end of the chain is red.
CLUE 2 One clip separates one color pair, 2 clips separate another color pair, and 3 clips separate the third color pair.
CLUE 3 A purple clip touches 2 clips of the same color.

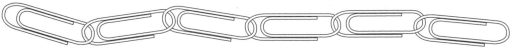

Clip-Clue Puzzles with Superfluous Clues
©Dale Seymour Publications

Clip-Clue Puzzle 107

Use 2 green clips, 2 yellow clips, 1 blue clip, and 1 white clip.

CLUE 1 Neither yellow clip touches the blue clip or the white clip.

CLUE 2 The blue clip does not touch the white clip.

CLUE 3 The yellow clip touches its mate.

CLUE 4 Neither end of the chain is blue.

Clip-Clue Puzzle 108

Use 2 orange clips, 2 white clips, and 2 red clips.

CLUE 1 The chain is not a repeating color pattern.

CLUE 2 A red clip is the third clip from one end of the chain.

CLUE 3 No clip touches a clip of its own color.

CLUE 4 Both white clips are second from an end.

Clip-Clue Puzzle 109

Use 2 yellow clips, 2 pink clips, 1 purple clip, and 1 blue clip.

CLUE 1 The purple clip is the third clip from one end.

CLUE 2 The chain contains a clip couple.

CLUE 3 A pink clip is between blue and purple.

CLUE 4 The blue clip is between yellow and pink.

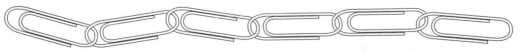

Clip-Clue Puzzle 110

Use 3 red clips, 2 white clips, and 1 blue clip.

CLUE 1 The chain contains exactly 2 clip couples.

CLUE 2 The blue clip is between 2 red clips.

CLUE 3 The ends of the chain are different colors.

CLUE 4 The chain does not contain 2 clip couples that touch.

Clip-Clue Puzzle 111

Use 4 orange clips, 2 blue clips, and 2 green clips.

CLUE 1 The chain contains a clip couple that is not orange.

CLUE 2 An orange clip touches both blue and green.

CLUE 3 The green clips are not parallel and the blue clips are not parallel.

CLUE 4 The chain contains a clip triple.

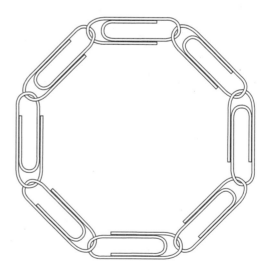

A Combination of Clip-Clue Puzzle Types

This section contains a mixture of four different clip-clue puzzle types. For each puzzle, decide which kind it is and solve it.

1. Some puzzles have a contradiction between the clues that makes the puzzle impossible to solve. Mark a large "X" through the first chain if the puzzle is impossible.

2. Some puzzles have just one chain that satisfies all the clues, and at the same time, all the given clues are necessary to find that unique solution. Solve these puzzles and color in your answer on the first chain.

3. Some puzzles have just one chain that satisfies all the clues, but one of the clues is superfluous. That clue is not needed because when all the other clues are combined, there is already just one solution. For these puzzles, find the unique solution, color it in on the first chain, and then circle the superfluous clue.

4. Some puzzles have two different chains that satisfy all the clues. For these puzzles, color in one solution on the first chain and the other solution on the second chain. (Be sure your chains are different, not just the same chain turned over or around.) Next write a clue that would make the first chain the unique solution to the puzzle, then write a clue that would make the second chain the unique solution.

Clip-Clue Puzzle 112

Use 2 green clips and 2 white clips.

CLUE 1 Each white clip touches only 1 green clip.

CLUE 2 The third clip from at least one end is white.

CLUE 3A _____

_____

CLUE 3B _____

_____

Clip-Clue Puzzle 113

Use 2 purple clips, 1 red clip, and 1 blue clip.

CLUE 1 The chain contains a clip couple.

CLUE 2 The red clip does not touch purple.

CLUE 3A _____

_____

CLUE 3A _____

_____

A Combination of Clip-Clue Puzzle Types

Clip-Clue Puzzle 114

Use 2 red clips, 1 orange clip, 1 brown clip, and 1 yellow clips.

CLUE 1 A red clip is separated from its mate by exactly 2 clips.

CLUE 2 The yellow clip does not touch red.

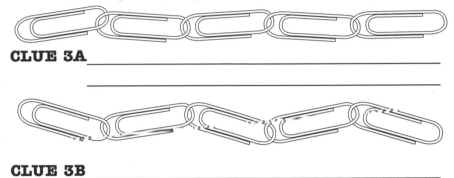

CLUE 3A _____

_____

CLUE 3B _____

_____

Clip-Clue Puzzle 115

Use 2 green clips, 2 yellow clips, and 1 blue clip.

CLUE 1 The blue clip is fourth from a yellow clip.

CLUE 2 The chain contains 2 clip couples.

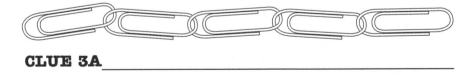

CLUE 3A _____

_____

CLUE 3B _____

_____

A Combination of Clip-Clue Puzzle Types

Clip-Clue Puzzle 116

Use 2 yellow clips, 2 blue clips, and 2 white clips.
CLUE 1 No clip touches a clip of its own color.
CLUE 2 The yellow clips are parallel to each other.

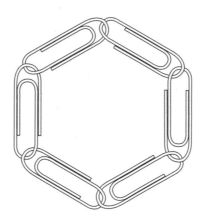

CLUE 3A_____

_____

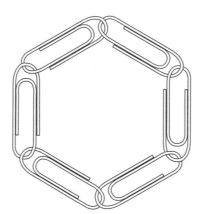

CLUE 3B_____

_____

Clip-Clue Puzzle 117

Use 2 blue clips and 2 purple clips.

CLUE 1 A blue clip is third from a purple clip.

CLUE 2 The chain contains no clip couples.

CLUE 3A_____

_____

CLUE 3B_____

_____

Clip-Clue Puzzle 118

Use 2 blue clips, 1 orange clip, and 1 red clip.

CLUE 1 The red clip does not touch the orange clip.

CLUE 2 Neither end of the chain is red.

CLUE 3A_____

_____

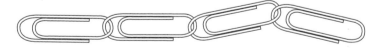

CLUE 3B_____

_____

Clip-Clue Puzzle 119

Use 2 red clips, 2 white clips, and 1 blue clip.

CLUE 1 The chain contains exactly 1 clip couple.

CLUE 2 The blue clip does not touch white.

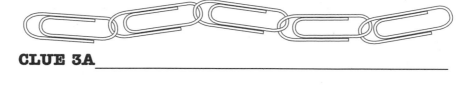

CLUE 3A_____

_____

CLUE 3B_____

_____

Clip-Clue Puzzle 120

Use 2 green clips and 2 orange clips.

CLUE 1 A green clip touches both green and orange.

CLUE 2 An orange clip touches both green and orange.

CLUE 3A_____

_____

CLUE 3B_____

_____

A Combination of Clip-Clue Puzzle Types

Clip-Clue Puzzle 121

Use 3 pink clips and 3 red clips.

CLUE 1 A red clip is parallel to a clip that touches 2 pink clips.

CLUE 2 The chain forms a repeating color pattern.

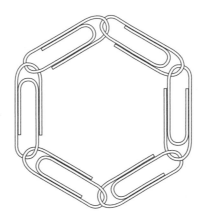

CLUE 3A _____

_____

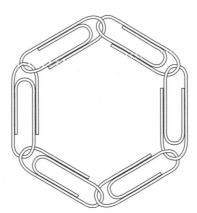

CLUE 3B _____

_____

Clip-Clue Puzzle 122

Use 2 yellow clips, 2 orange clips, and 1 white clip.

CLUE 1 One clip is the third clip from its color mate.

CLUE 2 The white clip is the fourth clip from an orange clip.

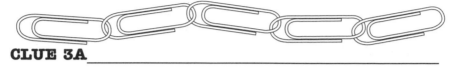

CLUE 3A _____

_____

CLUE 3B _____

_____

Clip-Clue Puzzle 123

Use 3 blue clips, 2 green clips, and 1 yellow clip.

CLUE 1 One blue clip touches both of the other blue clips.

CLUE 2 Neither end of the chain is green.

CLUE 3A _____

_____

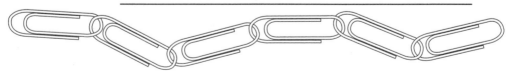

CLUE 3B _____

_____

A Combination of Clip-Clue Puzzle Types

Clip-Clue Puzzle 124

Use 2 white clips and 2 purple clips.

CLUE 1 A white clip touches 2 clips of the same color.

CLUE 2 A purple clip touches 2 clips of the same color.

CLUE 3A _____

_____

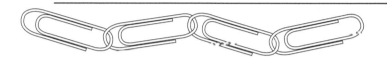

CLUE 3B _____

_____

Clip-Clue Puzzle 125

Use 3 blue clips, 2 red clips, and 1 green clip.

CLUE 1 The green clip touches 2 blue clips.

CLUE 2 Both red clips are between 2 blue clips.

CLUE 3A _____

_____

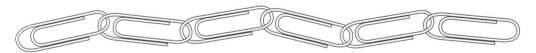

CLUE 3B _____

_____

A Combination of Clip-Clue Puzzle Types

Clip-Clue Puzzle 126

Use 4 blue clips and 4 orange clips.

CLUE 1 The chain is symmetric.

CLUE 2 An orange clip touches 2 orange clips.

CLUE 3 A blue clip couple touches 2 orange clips.

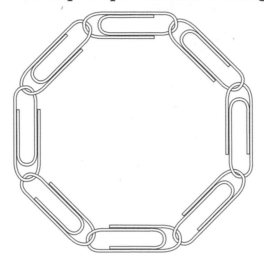

CLUE 4A _____

_____

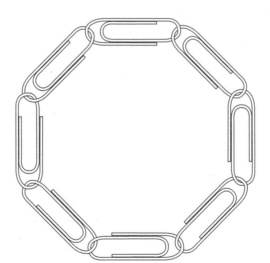

CLUE 4B _____

_____

Clip-Clue Puzzle 127

Use 2 orange clips, 1 pink clip, and 1 green clip.

CLUE 1 The pink clip is between an orange clip and a green clip.

CLUE 2 One end of the chain is green.

CLUE 3 The green clip touches an orange clip.

CLUE 4A _____

_____

CLUE 4B _____

_____

Clip-Clue Puzzle 128

Use 2 yellow clips and 2 orange clips.

CLUE 1 A yellow clip is between 2 orange clips.

CLUE 2 The chain is symmetric.

CLUE 3 One end of the chain is yellow.

CLUE 4A _____

_____

CLUE 4B _____

_____

A Combination of Clip-Clue Puzzle Types

Clip-Clue Puzzle 129

Use 2 blue clips and 2 white clips.

CLUE 1 The chain is not a repeating color pattern.

CLUE 2 The chain does not contain a white clip couple.

CLUE 3 A blue clip is second from at least one end.

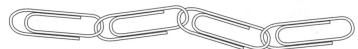

CLUE 4A_____

_____

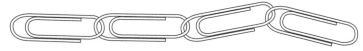

CLUE 4B_____

_____

Clip-Clue Puzzle 130

Use 2 red clips, 1 purple clip, 1 blue clip, and 1 yellow clip.

CLUE 1 The purple clip is between a red clip and the blue clip.

CLUE 2 The blue clip is between a red clip and the yellow clip.

CLUE 3 A red clip is between the blue clip and the yellow clip.

CLUE 4A_____

_____

CLUE 4B_____

_____

A Combination of Clip-Clue Puzzle Types

Clip-Clue Puzzle 131

Use 4 blue clips and 4 orange clips.

CLUE 1 An orange clip touches 2 blue clips.

CLUE 2 An orange clip touches 2 orange clips.

CLUE 3 A blue clip touches 2 blue clips.

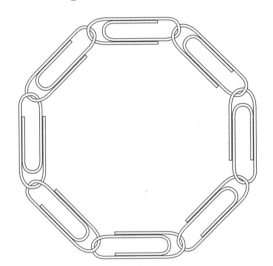

CLUE 4A_____

_____

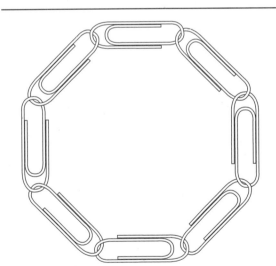

CLUE 4B_____

_____

A Combination of Clip-Clue Puzzle Types

Clip-Clue Puzzle 132

Use 2 white clips, 2 purple clips, and 1 orange clip.

CLUE 1 The white clips are equidistant from the center.
CLUE 2 The chain is not symmetric.
CLUE 3 The chain contains no clip couples.

CLUE 4A _____

_____

CLUE 4B _____

_____

Clip-Clue Puzzle 133

Use 2 yellow clips, 1 blue clip, and 1 green clip.

CLUE 1 Neither end of the chain is green.
CLUE 2 The blue clip touches yellow.
CLUE 3 A clip touches its color mate.

CLUE 4A _____

_____

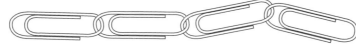

CLUE 4B _____

_____

A Combination of Clip-Clue Puzzle Types
©Dale Seymour Publications

Clip-Clue Puzzle 134

Use 2 green clips, 2 pink clips, and 2 red clips.

CLUE 1 The green clips are separated by at least 3 clips.

CLUE 2 The red clips are separated by exactly 2 clips

CLUE 3A_____

_____

CLUE 3B_____

_____

Clip-Clue Puzzle 135

Use 2 orange clips, 2 blue clips, and 2 yellow clips.

CLUE 1 Two different colored clips are each separated from their color mates by exactly 2 clips.

CLUE 2 The yellow clips are equidistant from the chain's middle.

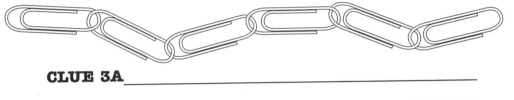

CLUE 3A_____

_____

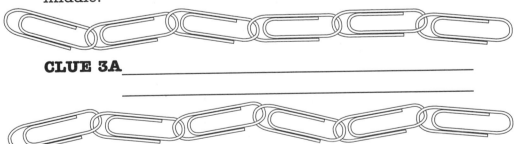

CLUE 3B_____

_____

A Combination of Clip-Clue Puzzle Types

Clip-Clue Puzzle 136

Use 4 orange clips, 2 blue clips, and 2 green clips.

CLUE 1 The chain has exactly 3 clip couples.

CLUE 2 The chain is symmetric.

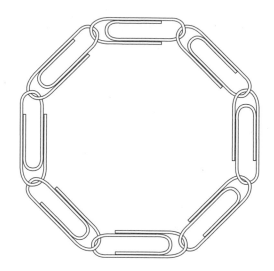

CLUE 3A_____

_____

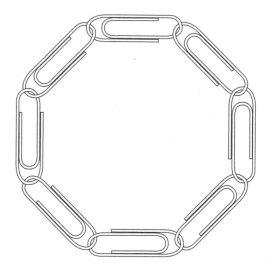

CLUE 3B _____

_____

A Combination of Clip-Clue Puzzle Types

Clip-Clue Puzzle 137

Use 2 white clips, 2 blue clips, and 2 red clips.

CLUE 1 A red clip touches a white clip.

CLUE 2 The chain is symmetric.

CLUE 3 A white clip is the fourth clip from at least one end.

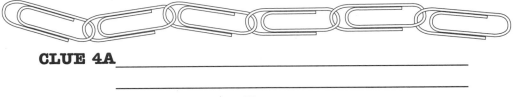

CLUE 4A _____

_____

CLUE 4B _____

_____

Clip-Clue Puzzle 138

Use 2 orange clips, 2 purple clips, and 1 red clip.

CLUE 1 A purple clip is separated from red by exactly 1 clip.

CLUE 2 An orange clip is separated from red by exactly 1 clip.

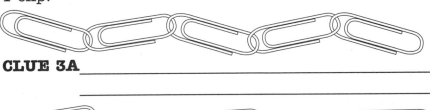

CLUE 3A _____

_____

CLUE 3B _____

_____

A Combination of Clip-Clue Puzzle Types

Clip-Clue Puzzle 139

Use 2 blue clips, 1 yellow clip, 1 pink clip, and 1 white clip.

CLUE 1 The white clip is third from a blue clip.

CLUE 2 The yellow clip is third from a blue clip.

CLUE 3 The pink clip does not touch the white clip.

CLUE 4A _____

_____

CLUE 4B _____

_____

Clip-Clue Puzzle 140

Use 2 purple clips, 1 red clip, 1 blue clip, and 1 green clip.

CLUE 1 The purple clips are equidistant from the ends.

CLUE 2 The blue clip is between purple and red.

CLUE 3 The green clip does not touch purple.

CLUE 4A _____

_____

CLUE 4B _____

_____

A Combination of Clip-Clue Puzzle Types

Clip-Clue Puzzle 141

Use 2 green clips, 2 blue clips, 2 yellow clips, and 2 red clips.

CLUE 1 The chain forms a repeating color pattern.

CLUE 2 A yellow clip touches blue.

CLUE 3 A green clip is the sixth clip from one of the blue clips.

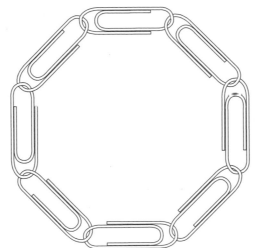

CLUE 4A _____

_____

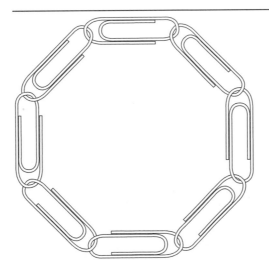

CLUE 4B _____

_____

A Combination of Clip-Clue Puzzle Types

Clip-Clue Puzzle 142

Use 3 red clips, 2 white clips, and 1 purple clip.

CLUE 1 The chain contains no clip couples.

CLUE 2 Two red clips are equal distance from the middle of the chain.

CLUE 3A _____

_____

CLUE 3B _____

_____

Clip-Clue Puzzle 143

Use 3 pink clips, 2 blue clips, and 1 orange clip.

CLUE 1 Both ends of the chain are the same color.

CLUE 2 Each blue clip is between a pink clip and an orange clip.

CLUE 3 A blue clip touches a pink clip couple.

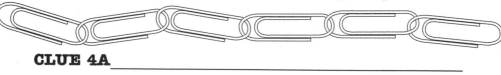

CLUE 4A _____

_____

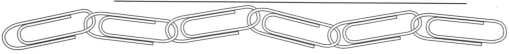

CLUE 4B _____

_____

A Combination of Clip-Clue Puzzle Types

Clip-Clue Puzzle 144

Use 1 orange, 1 green, 2 red, 2 pink, and 2 yellow clips.

CLUE 1 The green clip touches 2 clips of the same color.

CLUE 2 The first letters of the colors of 3 touching clips spell a verb in the order they appear.

CLUE 3 The yellow clips are parallel.

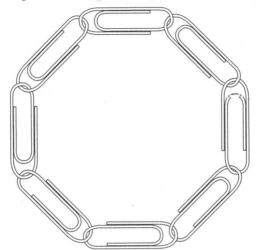

CLUE 4A _____

_____

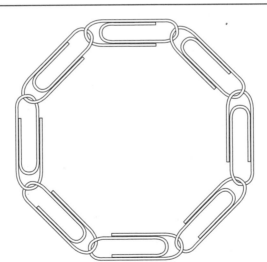

CLUE 4B _____

_____

A Combination of Clip-Clue Puzzle Types

Clip-Clue Puzzle 145

Use 2 blue clips, 2 green clips, and 1 white clip.

CLUE 1 The ends of the chain are the same color.

CLUE 2 The chain contains no clip couples.

CLUE 3 The chain is not symmetric.

CLUE 4A _____

_____

CLUE 4B _____

_____

Clip-Clue Puzzle 146

Use 3 yellow clips, 2 blue clips, and 1 orange clip.

CLUE 1 The chain contains exactly 2 clip couples.

CLUE 2 The orange clip does not touch yellow.

CLUE 3 At least one end of the chain is yellow.

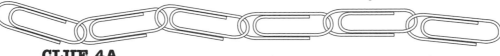

CLUE 4A _____

_____

CLUE 4B _____

_____

A Combination of Clip-Clue Puzzle Types
©Dale Seymour Publications

Clip-Clue Puzzle 147

Use 5 orange clips and 3 red clips.

CLUE 1 The chain is symmetric.

CLUE 2 The chain has exactly 2 clip couples.

CLUE 3 Every red clip is parallel to a clip that touches 2 orange clips.

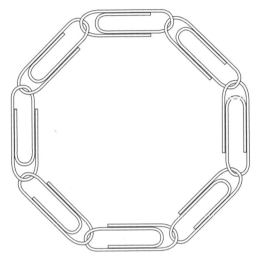

CLUE 4A _____

_____

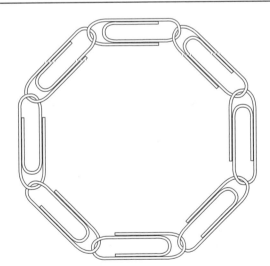

CLUE 4B _____

_____

Clip-Clue Puzzle 148

Use 2 red clips, 2 pink clips, and 2 green clips.

CLUE 1 Both halves of the chain contain a clip of each color.

CLUE 2 The 3 clips second, third, and fourth from either end contain a clip of each color.

CLUE 3 One of the 2 middle clips is red.

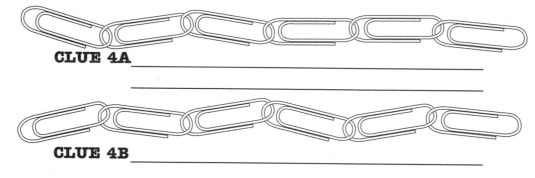

CLUE 4A _____

_____

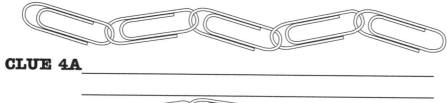

CLUE 4B _____

_____

Clip-Clue Puzzle 149

Use 2 blue clips, 1 pink clip, 1 purple clip, and 1 yellow clip.

CLUE 1 Neither end of the chain is blue.

CLUE 2 The purple clip is the third clip from the yellow.

CLUE 3 The chain contains no clip couples.

CLUE 4A _____

_____

CLUE 4B _____

_____

A Combination of Clip-Clue Puzzle Types

Clip-Clue Puzzle 150

Use 4 yellow clips and 4 orange clips.

CLUE 1 The chain contains a clip that does not touch a color mate.

CLUE 2 The chain is symmetric.

CLUE 3 The chain contains exactly 4 clip couples.

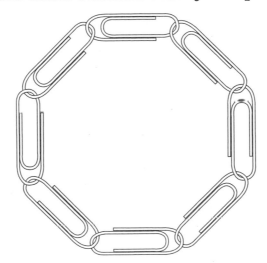

CLUE 4A _____

_____

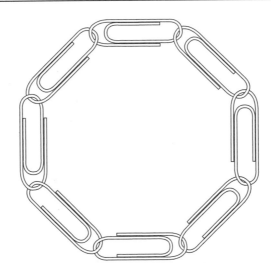

CLUE 4B _____

_____

A Combination of Clip-Clue Puzzle Types

Clip-Clue Puzzle 151

Use 2 blue clips, 2 white clips, and 2 red clips.

CLUE 1 One clip separates one color pair, 2 clips separate another color pair, and 3 clips separate the third color pair.

CLUE 2 A white clip touches 2 clips of the same color.

CLUE 3 Each red clip touches both a blue clip and a white clip.

CLUE 4A _____

_____

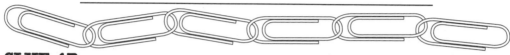

CLUE 4B _____

_____

Clip-Clue Puzzle 152

Use 2 purple clips, 1 pink clip, 1 yellow clip, and 1 blue clip.

CLUE 1 The purple clips are separated by at least 2 clips.

CLUE 2 The yellow clip does not touch the blue clip.

CLUE 3 The yellow clip is between the pink and the blue clips.

CLUE 4A _____

_____

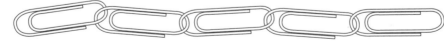

CLUE 4B _____

_____

A Combination of Clip-Clue Puzzle Types

Clip-Clue Puzzle 153

Use 4 green clips and 4 white clips.

CLUE 1 The chain contains exactly 4 clip couples.

CLUE 2 The chain is not symmetric

CLUE 3 The chain contains exactly 2 pairs of parallel color mates.

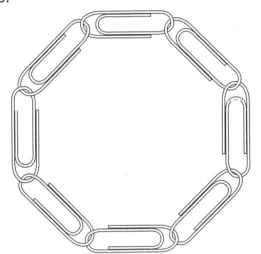

CLUE 4A _____

_____

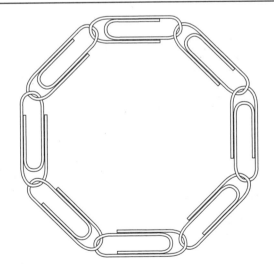

CLUE 4B _____

_____

Clip-Clue Puzzle 154

Use 2 yellow clips, 2 orange clips, and 2 white clips.

CLUE 1 The chain contains no clip couples.

CLUE 2 A clip and its color mate are equidistant from the center.

CLUE 3 Neither end of the chain is orange.

CLUE 4 Neither of the middle 2 clips is yellow.

CLUE 5A_____

_____

CLUE 5B_____

_____

Clip-Clue Puzzle 155

Use 2 red clips, 2 blue clips, and 1 pink clip.

CLUE 1 A red clip touches a blue clip.

CLUE 2 A red clip is separated from a blue clip by only 2 clips.

CLUE 3 A red clip is separated from a blue clip by 3 clips.

CLUE 4A_____

_____

CLUE 4B_____

_____

A Combination of Clip-Clue Puzzle Types

Clip-Clue Puzzle 156

Use 4 green clips and 4 purple clips.

CLUE 1 Exactly 2 pairs of clips are arranged so that the clips are parallel to a color mate.

CLUE 2 The chain contains exactly 4 clip couples.

CLUE 3 No green clip touches 2 green clips.

CLUE 4 No purple clip touches 2 purple clips.

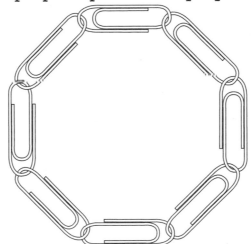

CLUE 5A _____

_____

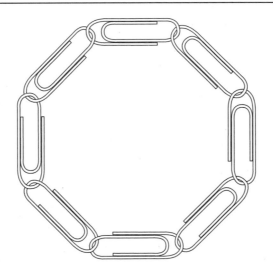

CLUE 5B _____

_____

A Combination of Clip-Clue Puzzle Types

Clip-Clue Puzzle 157

Use 4 orange clips, 2 yellow clips, and 2 red clips.

CLUE 1 Each yellow clip touches an orange clip couple or a red clip couple.

CLUE 2 Each red clip touches an orange clip couple or a yellow clip couple.

CLUE 3 Each red clip is parallel to a clip that touches 2 different colors.

CLUE 4 The chain is not symmetric.

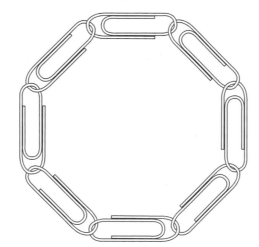

CLUE 5A_____

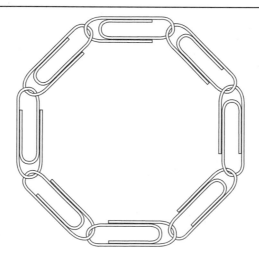

CLUE 5B_____

_____

A Combination of Clip-Clue Puzzle Types

Solutions to Clip-Clue Puzzles

The solutions are written in abbreviated form. The first letter of each color is used, "Pk" is used for pink to distinguish it from purple.

The answers for puzzles in the shape of pentagons, hexagons, and octagons are given linearly as the colors appear clockwise (or counterclockwise) around the figure from a random starting point. Remember that two chains are considered to be the same if one can be turned over or around to produce the other one.

For puzzles 52–81 and 112–157 the answers for written clues will vary; the given written clues are not the only possible answers. In every case the given clues do, however, represent examples of clues that do not make any preceding clues in the puzzles superfluous.

Clip-Clue Puzzles Plain and Simple

1.   Y Y G

2.   B W R

3.   O W B

4.   P B P P

5.   O R O

6.   Y O B Y

7.   B G B G

8.   O W O P

9.   R R Pk R

10.   B P B P

11.   G B B Y

12.   R O O R

13.   Pk W B W

14.   Y W R B

15.   Y G B Y

16.   B W R R

17.   Y O R O

18.   O O G W

19. R R Pk Pk

20. Y B B P

21. O W G Y

22. W Y B R

23. G P O P G

24. B P Pk Y

25. R Y O O R

26. O B P B O

27. G G W B B

28. B P W Pk

29. R R W B B W

30. O Y G Y G

31. W W B O B

32. R Pk W R Pk

33. Pk Y P B

34. W R W B W B W R

35. W W Y O O W

36. G G B B Y Y

37. P B B Pk B P

38. G G R R W R

39. B B O B O O B O

40. R B R R Y R

41. P W P P W B

42. B G G B G G

43. G P G O P G

44. B B B W R R

45. Y Y B P B P

46. W B O W B O

47. G R B R B G

48. O P Pk O P Pk

49. R W W B R B

50. W O Y O W Y

51. G G B G B Y G Y

Clip-Clue Puzzles with Insufficient Clues

52. Y Y R Y Y—The red clip is not second from either end.
     Y R Y Y Y—The center clip of the chain is yellow.

53. B B W W—The chain contains at least 1 clip couple.
     B W B W—A blue clip is between 2 white clips.

54.   Y G B G—Neither end of the chain is blue.

        B G Y G—The yellow clip is between 2 green clips.

55.   B B P P P—The 2 ends of the chain are not the same color.

        P B B P P—The middle clip is blue.

56.   W O W O R—Every orange clip touches a white clip.

        W W O O R—The chain contains at least 1 clip couple.

57.   Pk B Pk B B—Blue is not at both ends of the chain.

        B Pk Pk B B—The chain contains exactly 2 clip couples.

58.   Y B P P—The ends of the chain are not the same color.

        P Y B P—The purple clip does not touch its color mate.

59.   G G R W R—The white clip touches red.

        R R G W G—The white clip touches green.

60.   O W O O O O—The chain contains at least 4 connecting orange clips.

        O O W O O O—Every orange clip touches another orange clip.

61.   P B B P—At least 1 end clip is purple.

        B P P B—At least 1 end clip is blue.

62.   R R R W W W—The chain contains at least 1 clip couple.

        W R W R W R—Every red clip touches a white clip.

63.   G R R G—The ends of the chain are the same color.

        G R G R—One end of the chain is red.

64.   O W O W O—The white clip does not touch its color mate.

        O W W O O—The chain contains at least 1 clip couple.

65. B B B B Y Y—Every blue clip touches a blue clip.
B B B Y B Y—The yellow clips do not touch each other.

66. B O Y Y—The ends of the chain are different colors.
Y B O Y—The blue clip is not on an end.

67. R B R B—A red clip is between 2 blue clips.
R R B B—The chain contains at least 1 clip couple.

68. R W R W R W R W—A red clip touches 2 white clips.
R R W W R R W W—Every white clip touches a white clip.

69. Y G G Y G G—The ends of the chain are different colors.
G Y G G Y G—The chain is symmetric.

70. Pk B B B Pk—The chain contains at least 1 clip couple.
B Pk B Pk B—A pink clip is between 2 blue clips.

71. O O O R O O R R—A red clip touches a red clip.
O O O R O R O R—The chain is symmetric.

72. B O B B W—The middle clip is blue.
B B O B W—The orange and white clips are separated by just 1 clip.

73. P P R P B—The red clip is between 2 purple clips.
P P B P R—Neither end of the chain is blue.

74. B B B B B Y Y Y—The chain contains a clip triple.
B B Y B B Y B Y—A blue clip touches 2 yellow clips.

75. W Pk W O O O—The ends of the chain are not the same color.
W O O O Pk W—An orange clip is between 2 white clips.

76.	W R W R B R—The blue clip is second from one end.
	W R B R W R—The white clips are separated by more
		than 1 clip.

77.	B B B G G B G G—The chain is symmetric.
	G G B B G B G B—A green clip touches 2 blue clips.

78.	B P P B Y Y—The chain contains at least 2 clip
		couples.
	Y B P P B Y—The chain contains exactly 1 clip
		couple.

79.	O Y Y B O B—A yellow clip touches an orange clip.
	Y Y B O B O—At least one end of the chain is yellow.

80.	R Pk R G Pk G—The green clips are separated by
		exactly 1 clip.
	R G R Pk G Pk—The pink clips are separated by
		exactly 1 clip.

81.	W Y O O Y W—The chain contains no white clip that
		is second from an end.
	Y W O O W Y—The chain contains no yellow clip that
		is second from an end.

Clip-Clue Puzzles with Superfluous Clues

82.	R O W (clue 1)

83.	G P P G (clue 2)

84.	O Pk O B (clue 1)

85.	Y Y O O (clue 2)

86.	R W B R

87.	R G G G (clue 1)

88.   B Y G G (clue 1)

89.   W P W P

90.   R O B Pk

91.   Y B Y Y (clue 2)

92.   G R R O (clue 1)

93.   O B O W

94.   P P O P P (clue 1)

95.   B G G B G B G G (clue 2)

96.   Y Y Y O O O (clue 2)

97.   R W R Pk W R (clue 1)

98.   W Y B Y

99.   G O G G O G (clue 3)

100. R R W B B W

101. P P R Pk R P (clue 2)

102. Y G B B Y G (clue 1)

103. Y Y Y O Y Y O O (clue 3)

104. B O Pk O G B

105. B W R B R (clue 2)

106. R Pk P Pk R P

107. W G B G Y Y (clue 3)

108. O W O R W R (clue 2)

109. Pk B Pk P Y Y

110. W W R B R R (clue 2)

111. O O O G G O B B

A Combination of Clip-Clue Puzzle Types

112. G W W G

113. P P B R (clue 1)

114. X

115. B G G Y Y

116. Y B W Y W B—The chain is symmetric.
      Y B W Y B W—Each yellow clip touches 2 different
                  colors.

117. B P B P (clue 1)

118. O B R B

119. R B R W W—An end of the chain is white.
      B R W W R—Every white clip touches a red clip.

120. G G O O

121. X

122. W O Y Y O

123. B B B G G Y

124. W P W P (either clue 1 or 2)

125. B R R B G B

126. X

127. G O Pk O

128. X

129. W B B W (clue 3)

130. R P B R Y—The purple clip is not between the blue
 clip and the yellow clip.
 R B P R Y—The purple clip is between the blue clip
 and the yellow clip.

131. B B B O B O O O (clue 2)

132. P W P W O

133. X

134. G Pk R Pk G R—The chain does not contain any clip
 couples.
 G R Pk Pk R G—The chain is symmetric.

135. O Y B O Y B

136. X

137. B R W W R B

138. P P R O O—The chain contains at least 1 clip couple.
 P O R P O—The 2 orange clips are separated by at
 least 2 clips.

139. B B Pk Y W

140. P B G R P (clue 2)

141. G Y B R G Y B R (clue 2)

142. R W P R W R—The purple clip is between 2 white clips.
      R P W R W R—A red clip touches 2 white clips.

143. Pk Pk B B O Pk—The orange clip touches a pink clip.
      Pk Pk B O B Pk—The chain has a clip that touches 2
          clips of the same color.

144. Pk O Pk Y R G R Y

145. X

146. Y Y Y B O B

147. O O O R O R O R (clue 1)

148. R Pk G R Pk G—Neither green clip is second from an
          end.
      R G Pk R G Pk—Neither pink clip is second from an
          end.

149. X

150. Y Y Y O O Y O O—No orange clip is parallel to a clip
          that touches 2 orange clips.
      O O O Y Y O Y Y—No yellow clip is parallel to a clip
          that touches 2 yellow clips.

151. B R W R B W (clue 1)

152. B P Y Pk P

153. G G G W W W G W (clue 3)

154. Y W O W O Y

155. R Pk R B B—The pink clip does not touch both blue
       clips.
    R R B Pk B—The pink clip does not touch both red
       clips.

156. X

157. O O R Y O O R Y (clue 2)

Solutions to Clip-Clue Puzzles